BILLY **GRAHAM**

Evangelist to the World

BY MICHAEL CAPEK

CONTENT CONSULTANT
BILL J. LEONARD
DUNN PROFESSOR OF BAPTIST STUDIES AND
CHURCH HISTORY
SCHOOL OF DIVINITY, WAKE FOREST UNIVERSITY

Essential Library

An Imprint of Abdo Publishing | abdopublishing.com

abdopublishing.com

Published by Abdo Publishing, a division of ABDO, PO Box 398166, Minneapolis, Minnesota 55439. Copyright © 2019 by Abdo Consulting Group, Inc. International copyrights reserved in all countries. No part of this book may be reproduced in any form without written permission from the publisher. Essential Library™ is a trademark and logo of Abdo Publishing.

Printed in the United States of America, North Mankato, Minnesota
072018
092018

THIS BOOK CONTAINS
RECYCLED MATERIALS

Cover Photo: Jemal Countess/WireImage/Getty Images
Interior Photos: Bettmann/Getty Images, 4, 19, 46; Underwood Archives/Archive Photos/Getty Images, 9; AP Images, 13, 49, 54, 56, 60; Chuck Burton/AP Images, 14; Francis Miller/The LIFE Picture Collection/Getty Images, 22; Seth Poppel/Yearbook Library, 26; Frank Lilley/Express/Hulton Archive/Getty Images, 31; George Crouter/ The Denver Post/Getty Images, 32; Loomis Dean/Time & Life Pictures/The LIFE Picture Collection/Getty Images, 38, 42; Charles Mercer/AP Images, 64; Leslie Priest/ AP Images, 67; Anthony Camerano/AP Images, 69; Charles Tasnadi/AP Images, 74; John Rous/AP Images, 78; Arthur Schatz/The LIFE Picture Collection/Getty Images, 81; Gjon Mili/The LIFE Picture Collection/Getty Images, 86; Red Line Editorial, 92

Editor: Marie Pearson
Series Designer: Becky Daum

Library of Congress Control Number: 2018938202

Publisher's Cataloging-in-Publication Data

Names: Capek, Michael, author.
Title: Billy Graham: Evangelist to the world / by Michael Capek.
Other titles: Evangelist to the world
Description: Minneapolis, Minnesota : Abdo Publishing, 2019. | Series: Essential Lives | Includes online resources and index.
Identifiers: ISBN 9781532116117 (lib.bdg.) | ISBN 9781532157110 (ebook)
Subjects: LCSH: Graham, Billy (William Graham Jr. KBE), 1918-2018--Juvenile literature. | Evangelists--United States--Biography--Juvenile literature. | Baptists--United States--Clergy--Biography--Juvenile literature. | Evangelical Revival--Juvenile literature.
Classification: DDC 269.2092 [B]--dc23

CONTENTS

CHAPTER
ONE

"JUST AS I AM"

Fifteen-year-old Billy Graham was anything but happy when he heard that a series of revival meetings was coming to the town of Charlotte, North Carolina. During the summer of 1934, the Christian Men's Club decided to hold a revival meeting. This form of community religious campaign, often held in massive tents, had been a popular part of rural Southern culture for many years. The Great Depression, the worst financial crisis in American history, partially spurred the decision to hold the meeting. People were struggling to get by. Community leaders decided their town and region needed a spiritual boost.

Community leaders invited Dr. Mordecai Ham to conduct the 11-week campaign. He was famous for a loud and forceful style of preaching that graphically described the fires of Hell for non-Christians and the joys of Heaven for Christians. For the meetings, the Christian men of Charlotte constructed a huge wooden building with a sawdust-covered floor in a vacant lot

The Great Depression weighed heavily on many people in Charlotte, North Carolina. Textile workers held a strike when their hours were cut. The local union helped keep the workers fed during the strike.

downtown. People called it a tabernacle, a word used in the Bible's Old Testament to describe the movable tent the ancient Israelites used for worship. The sturdy, temporary building in Charlotte was large enough to seat between 4,000 and 5,000 people.[1]

Although Graham's father was one of the event organizers, Graham was unenthusiastic. After all, he was already a Christian, a member of the local Reformed Presbyterian Church. He had heard stories about Ham's flashy revival meetings and how the fiery evangelist

REVIVALISM IN THE UNITED STATES

Since the colonial period, which started in the late 1400s, revivals have been one way in which Christians have invited others to faith and membership in churches. Jonathan Edwards preached a sermon titled "Sinners in the Hands of an Angry God" in 1741. His graphic descriptions of the suffering of sinners in Hell caused many in New England to become outspoken about their faith in what is called the Great Awakening. The Second Great Awakening followed in the South at the beginning of the 1800s. At places such as Cane Ridge, Kentucky, in 1801, thousands responded to preachers' calls to accept Jesus Christ as their savior. A key figure in a northern revival during the 1830s was preacher Charles Grandison Finney, one of the first evangelists to offer an invitation for people to walk to what was called an anxious bench so Christians could pray for them. Revivalist Dwight L. Moody became a national celebrity in the late 1800s, preaching a simple Christian message packaged with comforting gospel music. In the early 1900s, showman-preacher Billy Sunday both entertained and converted millions with his pulpit antics and folksy message.

liked to excite people. The whole thing sounded like a religious circus to Graham. Many of his friends went, mostly out of curiosity. They urged Graham to come too. However, he preferred to spend his evenings quietly resting or hanging out with friends who shared his opinions about revivals and pushy preachers.

Seeing for Himself

Several weeks into the campaign, Graham heard that Ham had begun making claims in his sermons that students at the local high school were engaging in immoral activities. The attacks made Graham angry. He did not drink or smoke. He certainly never engaged in anything more than innocent kissing with the girls he dated. He decided to go to the makeshift tabernacle and find out for himself what the preacher was saying.

What he found when he went a few nights later surprised him. The sheer size of the building and congregation, as well as the stirring music and preaching, were unlike anything he had ever experienced. Ham's style of preaching was vastly different from what Graham heard at his church. Ham was loud and animated. He raged at his listeners, peering and pointing at them, waving his arms and punching the air. His posture and attitude were active and intensely confrontational.

Ham thundered about how people have an illness called sin. Sin is not living up to the moral standards God has set. People need to believe in Jesus Christ as the only cure. For the first time in his life, Graham heard preaching about Hell, the second coming of Jesus Christ, and the end of times on Earth. Despite his religious upbringing, these were new and startling concepts to him. Particularly troubling were the preacher's repeated assertions that only God knew the timetable. There was a cosmic ticking clock, and the alarm could go off at any moment. An immediate decision was necessary if humans hoped to avoid spending the rest of their lives in the fires of Hell, Ham kept insisting.

Graham felt sharp pangs of guilt and fear as he listened. Yet when the chords of the invitational hymn were sung, Graham made no move to join the throngs of others who went forward to accept Jesus Christ as their savior. The invitation is the moment when a preacher addresses those in the audience who feel sorrow for their sins and wish to become Christians. The preacher asks them to show their desire publicly by raising a hand or coming to the front of the congregation. Those who

Revival meetings often attracted large crowds.

wish to convert, which in this case means changing from being a non-Christian to a Christian, follow the preacher's instructions. They do this to show their desire to change their thinking and behavior to be in line with God's.

Graham went back night after night. "I would feel a stirring in my breast that was both pleasant and scary," he said, but he still found he simply could not budge from his seat.[2] During one service, Ham pointed suddenly in his direction and shouted, "You're a sinner!" Graham instinctively ducked behind the large hat of a woman sitting in front of him.[3] To avoid the searching eyes of the evangelist, Graham decided to join the revival choir. He had a terrible singing voice, but at least the choir was placed more comfortably, or so he assumed, behind the preacher's back. His friend Grady Wilson also joined him. In the choir, too, was J. D. Prevatte, a local businessman and friend of the Graham family. Prevatte had been watching the teen's spiritual struggles with particular interest.

Making a Decision

On November 1, 1934, six days before Graham's sixteenth birthday, the choir started singing the invitational hymn "Just as I Am." Prevatte stepped to Graham's side. "Billy Frank? Wouldn't you like to become a Christian?" Graham nodded and nudged Wilson in the ribs. "So why don't you boys settle it?" Prevatte asked. "I'll go down with you."[4]

As Graham later described in his autobiography, "I walked down to the front, feeling as if I had lead weights attached to my feet, and stood in the space before the platform." Prevatte stood beside him and explained the process of salvation in a simple way. But committing himself to Christ was not simple, he found. "The final issue was whether I would turn myself over to [God's] rule in my life."[5] As Graham stood there, he considered how he had grown up in a Christian home. He could recite from memory many Bible verses his parents had made him learn. He had been baptized and confirmed as a child in his family's church. Weren't those demonstrations of his faith enough? Then he realized those had been decisions made by his parents, not by him. This time, the decision was his alone. That night, Graham made his own decision to commit himself to Christ.

On the same night, 300 or 400 others went forward, too.[6] Graham noticed that many were weeping, and some even shouted for joy. Oddly, he felt very little emotion. "No bells went off inside of me," he wrote later. "No signs flashed across the tabernacle ceiling. No physical

INFLUENTIAL HYMN

Religious magazine editor Charlotte Elliott wrote the poem "Just as I Am" in 1835. Arranged to a melody composed by William B. Bradbury in 1849, it quickly became one of the most frequently sung invitational songs at fundamentalist churches and evangelistic meetings in the United States, including Graham's. "Just as I Am" was also the title Graham chose for his 1997 best-selling autobiography. The song begins:

Just as I am, without one plea,

But that Thy blood was shed for me,

And that Thou bid'st me come to Thee,

O Lamb of God, I come! I come![7]

palpitations made me tremble." Instead, he mainly felt relieved, "quiet, not delirious. Happy and peaceful."[8]

Later at home, alone in the quiet of his own room, "I went to my bed and for the first time in my life got down on my knees without being told to do so." He felt compelled to speak directly to God but found he did not know exactly what to say. "I don't know what happened to me tonight," he prayed finally. "*You* know. And I thank You for the privilege I've had tonight."[9]

That night in 1934 set Graham on a path that led him far beyond rural North Carolina. To say his impact on world religion was profound would be an understatement. Graham preached the gospel of Jesus Christ to more people in person than anyone in history did. The gospel is the message that Jesus Christ, the Son of God, became a man and lived a perfect life. Christians believe Jesus then died to pay the penalty of human sins and rose again so people who accept Jesus as their savior can be forgiven and live with God forever. Graham reached 215 million people in more than 185 countries and territories. Hundreds of millions heard him speak on the radio, on television, in films, and on webcasts. Many more read some of his 33 books, several of which were best sellers.[10] He preached to

Young Graham had no idea that his decision to accept Jesus as his savior would soon lead him to a lifetime of influence around the world.

and counseled presidents and world leaders, including kings and queens. The story of how a simple farm boy rose from humble beginnings to become whom some have called America's Pastor is, like the man himself, uniquely American.

CHAPTER
TWO

BILLY FRANK

William Franklin Graham Jr. was born on November 7, 1918, in the family's Charlotte farmhouse. Siblings Catherine, Melvin, and Jean arrived over the next 14 years. From an early age, Billy Frank, as family and friends called him, was in almost constant motion. He was always rushing about, knocking things off shelves and tables. His mother was relieved when he finally started school. While classmates remembered Graham as fun and likable, teachers mostly recalled him as a disturbance.

Given his workload on the farm and inability to sit still, young Graham was not a stellar student, even in high school. He had trouble memorizing things and preferred the open woods and fields to a confined classroom. In his teen years, Graham's energy found an outlet in sports, mainly baseball and basketball. He was known for his piercing blue eyes, blond hair, handsome face, dazzling smile, and outgoing, playful personality. All of these traits made him immensely popular.

People can visit Graham's childhood home, *left*, at the Graham Family Homeplace.

Like most people in their region during the Great Depression, the Grahams were a Christian family. They regularly attended church and prayed and read the Bible as a family every day. Graham, however, thought religion and church were mostly boring. In 1934, Graham's father hosted an outdoor prayer meeting at the farm. Irritated by the noise and singing, Graham told one of the hired hands that the gathering was "some fanatics" his father had allowed onto the property. But his father recalled later that someone during that meeting had loudly prayed, "O Lord! Out of this very city . . . may you raise up such a one as will go out and preach Your gospel to the ends of the earth!"[1]

During high school, Graham had no idea what he would do with his life. He and his family assumed he would continue working on the family farm and perhaps inherit it one day. No doubt he would get married after he graduated. Whatever line of work he chose, he vowed he would

MOST POPULAR

Graham's lanky frame was always dressed in the latest styles. His snappy appearance and charismatic personality made him immensely popular, particularly with girls. Graham's younger sister Catherine recalled that in his teen years, her brother "was always in love with a different girl every day. He really did like the girls. And they liked him."[2]

never become a mortician or a preacher. He found both of those professions equally unpleasant.

However, at age 15, such decisions seemed far in the future. That summer, Graham's keenest interests were playing baseball and careening around town and countryside in his father's Plymouth sedan. Driver's licensing and traffic-law enforcement in the rural South were lax. Graham drove all over without much oversight.

Despite his seemingly carefree life, during the summer of 1934, Graham began to feel a growing sense of restlessness. His family's drab, steadfast religious practices frustrated him. He felt stifled, almost buried alive in rural North Carolina. He wanted to travel, to see and experience the wider world beyond his small town and isolated farm. Feeling trapped, he played and worked harder and drove faster and farther than he should have. "I just know that I kept feeling that something was going to happen to me," Graham later told writer Marshall Frady. "Something was about to happen to take me out of all that, out of the farm and out of Charlotte."[3]

After Revival

In the days and weeks following his spiritual conversion, Graham wondered what, exactly, had happened to him. He felt changed. Church activities, which he had always found dull, suddenly seemed fresh and exciting. He felt compelled to take notes during his pastor's sermons, and he began to read the Bible. He found himself singing hymns while he milked the cows. He felt his conversion ought to be signaled by some sort of outward sign. He began to insist everyone call him simply Billy, without the Frank.

One year later, a team of young evangelists came to Charlotte for a series of revival meetings. They were lively and fun to be around. One of them, Jimmie Johnson, stayed at the Graham house. One afternoon, Johnson asked Graham to drive with him to a nearby town where he was scheduled to preach in a city jail. While Johnson was explaining what salvation meant to a dozen men behind bars in a jail cell, he suddenly turned to Graham. "Here's a fellow who'll tell you what it's like to be converted."[4]

Graham hated speaking publicly, and he had never told anyone outside his family about his faith. Somehow,

Graham graduated from Sharon High School in Charlotte.

he stammered through his testimony, or his story about how he became a Christian. Johnson told him afterward that he had done well, but Graham was not convinced. He had seen only boredom and indifference in the faces of the prisoners. The unsettling experience only confirmed what he had always felt. He would never become a preacher.

Salesman

Despite this experience, after Graham graduated high school in 1936, he enrolled at Bob Jones College (BJC), a Bible school in Tennessee. That summer, Graham asked Grady Wilson and several other boys he knew to join him selling Fuller Brush cleaning brushes door-to-door. Graham's youthful enthusiasm and sincere smile brought him quick success. After reading the promotional material that came with his sales case full of sample brushes, Graham became almost as sold on selling brushes as he was on his religious faith. By the

THE FULLER BRUSH MAN

When Alfred Fuller started his own business in 1906, he felt God had called him for a special purpose. That purpose turned out to be selling brushes, a different brush for scrubbing everything from bathtubs to battleships. Fuller perfected the art of door-to-door selling and supplied each recruit in his army of traveling salesmen with a booklet explaining his foolproof methods. Getting one's foot in the door was more than a saying to Fuller. It was step one in his manual. During the Great Depression, when selling anything was next to impossible, Fuller Brush salesmen like Graham still thrived. The genius of Fuller's method was his ability to infect employees with his own evangelistic spirit and channel that energy toward selling a commercial product. The business model and techniques Fuller pioneered inspired multitudes of successful people over the years, no matter what product they were selling. Graham never said so, but the nonprofit Graham later founded, the Billy Graham Evangelistic Association, successfully applied many of Fuller's original principles.

end of summer, he had sold more Fuller brushes and earned more money than anyone else in the North and South Carolina region. The experience taught him a great deal about other people and himself. "Sincerity," Graham said later, "is the biggest part of selling anything, including the Christian plan of salvation."[5]

People often called Graham, Wilson, and the other young men selling brushes the "Preacher Boys" because of their Christian faith and because nearly all, except Graham, had decided they wanted to become ministers one day.[6] The friends ate and roomed together as they traveled. They read the Bible, prayed, and occasionally even preached on street corners together.

Most of the boys loved giving sidewalk sermons, but Graham did not. Wilson said, "He couldn't even give a sensible testimony."[7] In the fall, Graham and Wilson traveled together to BJC full of hope that their personal destinies would soon be revealed to them. Whatever it was, for Graham, it seemed as though it definitely would not be preaching.

CHAPTER
THREE

"YOU'VE GOT ME"

B JC turned out to be one of the worst experiences of Graham's life. He found the whole atmosphere at BJC cold and strict. Socializing, and especially dating, were essentially forbidden. Rigorous study and self-discipline were the school's major emphases. Fun and recreation in any form was viewed as time wasted and were strongly discouraged. So was class discussion. At BJC, teachers taught and students listened. Graham was curious by nature, but any student who dared to question a teacher at BJC was labeled insubordinate and disruptive. Graham was always in trouble academically and behaviorally. He lost weight, did not sleep well, and was often sick. By midterm, he knew he would have to find a school better suited to his own temperament.

In early 1937, on the advice of his family doctor, Graham finally found his place at Florida Bible Institute (FBI), a school for training ministers near Tampa, Florida. Warm and welcoming, FBI had barely 75 students.[1] Teachers were like counselors and classes were

BJC had many rules for its students, including mandatory group prayer.

BOB JONES VS. BILLY GRAHAM

Graham and BJC founder and president Bob Jones Sr. developed a bitter disagreement over the years after Graham left BJC. The cause was the same issue that divided fundamentalist Christians during that period—ecumenism. This is the belief that no specific denomination is the only correct version of Christianity. Graham embraced ecumenism early. Jones and others preached that any belief other than their own narrow brand was not biblical. Traditional fundamentalists such as Jones refused to tolerate ecumenism. Graham mostly refused to respond to the criticism. But until the day he died in 1968, Jones continued to lead attacks against Graham and his ministry. The fundamentalist fight still rages today.

informal Bible study groups. He still did not excel gradewise, but he had always learned far more outside of confined spaces than in them.

Despite the excitement and sense of belonging he felt at FBI, Graham still could not convince himself that God was calling him to preach the gospel full time. Insomnia, a problem that plagued him throughout most of his life, only added to his restlessness. Graham roamed the campus many nights and canoed on the adjacent river. He sometimes practiced preaching in the blackness to alligators and cypress stumps but did not feel he could do it before a human audience.

Bible students at FBI were often assigned to preach at local churches when their ministers were away or ill. In the spring of 1937, FBI's Dean John Minder told Graham that he was sending him to a Baptist church in northern Florida. He had been assigned to preach there the very next night. Stunned, Graham argued and begged. He had never preached a real sermon in his life. He needed more time. The dean simply laughed and assured him he would be praying for him.

Graham spent the entire night and all of the next day writing, praying, and practicing. He could not decide what topic to preach on, so he prepared four complete sermons. He took the outlines of all four with him when he left for the worship service. At tiny Bostwick Baptist Church, a congregation of approximately 40 gathered to hear the lanky, nervous young student preach. Trembling and sweating, Graham launched into sermon number one, but quickly bogged down. He switched to outline number two, and then, in quick succession, to sermons three and four. He finished and sat down, only to realize he had preached for a total of only eight minutes.

He was certain now. He was definitely not cut out for the pulpit. Yet he still could not escape the feeling that God was calling him for some specific purpose.

Graham's years at FBI were a pivotal time in his life.

He did not know exactly what that purpose was, but others, including his academic and personal adviser Minder, suspected that preaching was exactly what Graham was destined to do. Minder kept encouraging Graham, pushing him to keep praying, studying, and honing his preaching skills.

Changing Direction

At about that time, Graham fell in love with a girl named Emily Cavanaugh. She was deeply spiritual and beautiful. Not long after they started dating, Graham asked Cavanaugh to marry him. She accepted, and then soon after she changed her mind. She had fallen for one of Graham's friends. Besides, Graham's boundless, unfocused energy made her feel uncomfortable, even a little frightened. His romantic dreams dashed, Graham began to suffer through a period of deep depression. Graham's insomnia grew worse. He poured out his misery to his friend and adviser, Minder, who prayed with him as he wept for hours.

It was obvious to Minder, if not to Graham, that the root of his suffering was more than just the end of a youthful romance. He was "struggling with the Holy Spirit over the call of God to be a minister," Graham wrote of himself years later. "That was the last thing I wanted to be, and I used all kinds of rationalizations to convince God to let me do something else."[2] He took to roaming the city streets and the fairways of a nearby golf course, praying and crying. It was on the fairways, late one night, that he finally fell to his knees. "All right,

Lord. If you want me, you've got me. I'll be what you want me to be and I'll go where you want me to go."[3]

In that moment, everything changed, Graham later wrote. "No sign in the heavens. No voice from above. But in my spirit, I knew I had been called to the ministry. And I knew my answer was yes."[4]

After that night, all of his priorities, objectives, and energies shifted. Graham began to study and practice obsessively. He could barely sleep at night. Now, however, it was not despair, but excitement keeping him awake. He accepted every opportunity to preach, continually honing his style and skills.

One thing Graham avoided as long as possible during his early evolution from student to preacher was giving an official invitation. Offering a call to salvation at an evangelistic meeting, after all, offered risks. What if no one responded? Not only would it be a serious blow to his ego, it might be

The first time Graham's younger sister Catherine heard him preach in a small church, she was astonished and embarrassed. "He was preaching so loud, waving his arms around," she once told biographer Marshall Frady. She whispered to a friend sitting with her, "What in the world has come over him? He's preaching like he thinks he's preaching to ten thousand people."[5]

interpreted as a sign that maybe God had not called him after all. So he was extremely nervous the first time he offered an official invitation. It was at the end of a sermon to a congregation of approximately 100 in Venice, Florida. To his relief, 32 people came forward.[6]

Later in the summer of 1938, Graham was invited for the first time to preach at a youth revival at East Palatka Baptist Church. Still only a teenager himself, Graham was stunned night after night as youth and adults alike flooded forward in response to his invitations. A local paper wrote that it was the "greatest meeting in the history of the church."[7] That revival, Graham said later, was the first time he began to think that perhaps large-scale evangelism, as opposed to a single church ministry, might be his true calling.

During that revival, leaders in the church were dismayed to learn the fiery young evangelist was a Presbyterian, not a Baptist. Not only was he the wrong denomination, they told him, he had not been baptized in the proper Baptist manner. Baptism is a ritual practice observed by most Christians. Babies or new converts are ceremonially cleansed with water. Graham had been sprinkled with water as a baby and again, later, when he was confirmed, based on that church's faith and catechism. But he had never been fully immersed in a pool of water in a ceremony performed by an ordained Baptist minister. Of course, the ritual was not necessary for salvation, the minister explained. But if Graham intended to keep preaching in Baptist churches, he would have to comply with their customs and requirements.

Graham prayed about it. Eventually, although he personally felt the ceremony was unnecessary, he could see no reason why he should not be baptized for a third time. In late 1938, Graham joined a group of his own recent converts and was baptized in a nearby lake by the

RUTH BELL GRAHAM

Born in China to American missionary parents, Ruth Bell intended to go back there as a missionary as soon as she graduated from Wheaton. Intelligent, strong-willed, and deeply religious, she fell as hard for Graham's habit of praying regularly and bold preaching style as she did for his good looks. She was troubled, though, knowing that marriage would almost certainly mean the end of her dream of missionary work. She also guessed correctly how difficult life would be married to a man whose first priority would always be service to God. "If I marry Bill," she wrote in a 1941 journal entry, "I must marry him with my eyes open. He will be increasingly burdened for lost souls and increasingly active in the Lord's work. After the joy and satisfaction of knowing that I am his by rights—and his forever, I will slip into the background. . . . In short, be a lost life. Lost in Bill's."[8] Not long after, she wrote this: "Lord, if you let me serve you with that man, I'd consider it the greatest privilege of my life."[9]

Ruth and Graham valued their time together at home, but life was often busy.

local pastor. In February 1939, Graham was officially ordained as a minister in the local Baptist association.

Graham graduated from FBI in May 1940 with a degree in theology, and almost immediately, he enrolled at Wheaton College near Chicago, Illinois. At Wheaton, he studied anthropology for a bachelor's degree. He also met Ruth Bell. After a good deal of consideration on her part, they were married in August 1943, in Montreat, North Carolina, soon after their graduation.

CHAPTER
FOUR

YOUTH FOR CHRIST

Beginning in January 1944, Graham accepted
an offer to preach on live radio. Part music and
part evangelism, *Songs in the Night* was a 45-minute
show broadcast every Sunday night from the basement
of Western Springs Baptist Church, approximately
20 miles (32 km) south of Wheaton.[1] Besides Graham,
the broadcast featured the talents of religious music
star and early Youth for Christ (YFC) organizer George
Beverly Shea. YFC aimed to attract young people to
Christianity. Graham learned a lot from *Songs in the
Night*, particularly the power of media to reach vast
audiences. It would later sprout into one of the most
far-reaching radio and television broadcast ventures
in history.

Leading a Rally

However, nothing Graham had experienced previously
affected him more than his experience at the 1944
Chicagoland YFC rally. That was Graham's first taste of

George Beverly Shea, *left*, was a singer and composer nominated ten
times for Grammy Awards. He won a Grammy in 1965 and received a
Lifetime Achievement Grammy in 2010.

large-scale evangelism. It was also the beginning of an exciting new chapter in his life.

It was May 27, 1944. That night, Graham paced backstage at Orchestra Hall in downtown Chicago, anxiously biting his nails. Out front, waiting for him to speak, was a crowd of more than 2,500, mostly teens and young members of the military.[2] The event was the first Chicagoland YFC rally held by Chicago YFC. Begun in New York City in 1940, YFC chapters had already formed in many large cities in the East. By 1944, the evangelistic ministry was taking the central United States by storm. Graham had been asked to deliver the sermon, and he was suffering terrible stage fright.

He had never spoken to such a large audience before. And it bothered him that some event planners had objected that Graham, and not someone better known, had been selected to preach the first sermon. Of course, they were right. He was just out of college and had limited experience. Still, Torrey Johnson, YFC's president, had heard Graham preach. Johnson was convinced Graham's energetic style and biblical message were exactly what the expanding YFC program needed. He had overruled everyone else's objections. Graham had accepted the invitation, but now that the time had come for him to speak, Graham was still teetering between feeling honored and overwhelmed.

As soon as he began to speak, though, his qualms vanished. He felt a lightness and freedom, and the message he prepared flowed effortlessly while the previously raucous crowd sat transfixed in silence. When Graham gave the invitation prompting those wishing to accept Jesus as their savior to come forward, 40 people responded.[3]

After that event, preaching invitations poured in. He began appearing regularly at Chicago YFC meetings and others around the country. Hired as YFC's first official field representative, he traveled around the nation, preaching at YFC meetings and helping organize local chapters. That year, he traveled some

"GEARED TO THE TIMES"

"Geared to the Times, Anchored to the Rock."[4] The longtime motto of YFC summarizes the philosophy behind the organization. Created as a way to minister to servicemen and servicewomen during World War II (1939–1945), YFC soon evolved into a youth phenomenon. YFC's main appeal was that it was nothing like going to church. There were games, ventriloquists, magicians, and silly skits. Music was upbeat and loud. Ministers were always young and enthusiastic, usually dressed in brightly colored suits and neon ties. Sermons were short and relevant to teen concerns and current issues. The group worked to convince teens that Christianity was not dark and dusty, but alive and important.

135,000 miles (217,000 km) and was designated by United Airlines as its top nonmilitary passenger.[5]

YFC expanded worldwide. In 1946, Graham and fellow evangelist Charles Templeton traveled to the United Kingdom on a six-month campaign to spread the YFC fervor. Graham saw terrible devastation from World War II (1939–1945). During that tour, Graham preached at 360 meetings across several cities and organized active YFC chapters in many of them.[6] In early 1947, Graham returned home exhausted but filled with more excitement than he had ever felt.

At that point, he had not seen his wife Ruth and baby daughter Virginia, born in 1945, in more than six months. It strained the family's relationship. In 1947, the path of Graham's life and ministry took a detour.

ABSENTEE FATHER

Billy and Ruth Graham had five children: Virginia, Anne, Ruth, Franklin, and Nelson. Graham said in his autobiography that while his children were growing up he was "on the road at least one fourth of the time."[7] Another time, he said he was away from home 60 percent of the time.[8] It is not clear exactly which figure is more accurate.

College President

Years earlier, Graham had met Dr. W. B. Riley, founder and president of

Northwestern Schools, a Minneapolis, Minnesota, Bible college. Riley heard Graham preach and afterward approached him with a proposition. Riley told him he was terminally ill, and he wanted Graham to replace him as president of the college when he died. Graham told Riley he had no real educational training. Besides, at that time he was busy doing large-scale YFC evangelism. Riley was so insistent, however, that Graham finally agreed to take the position on an interim basis, in case of emergency. That emergency arrived in December 1947 when Riley died. In 1948, at age 29, Graham became the youngest college president in the nation. His second daughter, Anne, was also born that year.

Graham spent most of his time in Minnesota performing administrative duties for Northwestern Schools until he left the school in 1952. He also preached at YFC meetings and was paid for conducting revival services, some of them quite large, around the country. Whenever he could, he went home to North Carolina, where Ruth was raising their growing family alone.

CHAPTER
FIVE

THE CANVAS CATHEDRAL

While president of Northwestern Schools, Graham conducted several citywide gospel campaigns in 1947 that were important for several reasons. Those events marked the first time Graham and his full team of salaried associates worked together. These primary people would soon form the bedrock of the Billy Graham Evangelistic Association (BGEA). The musical talent of the team included emcee and choir director Cliff Barrows and his wife, Billie, who played the organ and piano, as well as soloist George Beverly Shea. Grady Wilson, now an ordained minister, was Graham's first associate evangelist.

The citywide campaigns of 1947 were also important because they tested and established the plan the association would follow again in years to come. That plan was fourfold. First was an all-out effort to get as many local churches as possible, as early as possible, participating in the planning of a campaign. Next was to stress prayer as a constant unifying force among all aspects of the planning. Third, the team made every effort to ensure money was never an issue. Donations and offerings were acceptable, but outright begging or prodding was avoided. Fourth was to use local media for publicity and to make sure advertising was honest and sincere, never sensational or exaggerated.

THE MODESTO MANIFESTO

Early on, Graham became concerned about public perceptions of him and his ministry. He knew unscrupulous people were preaching the gospel, too, and some were taking advantage of people's faith and trust. He witnessed firsthand how easily a minister of the gospel could become entangled in sexual or financial scandals. In 1948, in an effort to sidestep pitfalls in their rapidly expanding ministry, Graham and his associates drew up a set of guidelines they agreed to follow. Drafted in Modesto, California, they called the list the "Modesto Manifesto."[1] Rule one was that none of the men could ever be alone with a woman other than their wives. Rule two had to do with financing. Donations could be requested and accepted, but money must never become their primary object. If God wanted them to continue, he would supply the funds. Once the BGEA was officially established in 1950, all money was handled by the organization. Graham and his team of associates received a set salary, not a percentage of the total amount received in a given city. Rule three involved humility. They would not advertise their own accomplishments, particularly their own estimates of attendance numbers or of those who made decisions to accept Christ at their events.

Los Angeles

After the campaigns of 1947, Graham and his associates received an invitation to try out their master plan on one of the biggest stages in the United States: Los Angeles, California. After a full year of planning and preparation, the Christ for Greater Los Angeles campaign began in early October 1949. The Ringling Bros. Circus leased a huge tent for the meetings. The press labeled the 6,000-seat tent "the Canvas Cathedral." Bright banners hanging on various sides beckoned visitors, announcing "Hear America's Sensational Young Evangelist!" and "Dazzling Array of Gospel Talent!"[2]

Despite the tent's circusy appearance, Graham and his team of associates did everything they could to make sure the services inside it were dignified and spiritual. There were celebrity guests and musical performers, but everything else was under the control and guidance of Graham and his team of associates. Graham and his gospel message were the featured event every night.

By 1949, Graham had come close to perfecting a unique set of physical and vocal gestures that became trademarks of his preaching style. They appeared natural and spontaneous, but were, in fact, the result of his

Graham's animation at the Los Angeles rallies caught listeners' attention.

years of practice on the YFC circuit, hours of planning and rehearsal, and close study of recordings of his previous sermons. One in particular caught the attention of reporters. Graham picked out specific individuals and glowered, pointed, and shouted, directly at them. His rapid thundering and double-pointed fingers, reporters said, made Graham sometimes look like he was shooting at his audience. One newspaper dubbed him "God's Machine Gun."[3]

Strategy and Attention

However, there was far more to Graham's sermons than mere theatrics. His messages at the Los Angeles campaign followed a careful intellectual pattern, a four-step formula he practiced for years. Graham began by citing alarming statistics or listing serious issues facing people in their daily lives. Second, he made frequent references to dire current events in the news—natural disasters, crime, scandal, war, Communism, nuclear weapons. Next, he would cite Scripture, prefaced by his favorite phrase, "The Bible says."[4] The passages he selected always seemed to prophesy, or foretell, the evils he was describing were, in fact, signs of impending doom. Once he sufficiently alerted his audience that Earth was hurtling

ON THE WIRE

Before microphones, revivalists had to speak loudly. Their messages were short because they would lose their voices. Microphones enabled revivalists to speak longer. As Graham grew in popularity, a microphone pinned to his jacket lapel amplified his already-powerful voice. The tent had loudspeakers positioned inside and outside. Long before the days of wireless microphones, music director Cliff Barrows sat behind the pulpit and constantly played out and reeled in wire as Graham strode around the platform. Some observers estimated the evangelist walked at least 1 mile (1.6 km) during every sermon.[5]

toward fiery destruction, he would advance to the last step—the invitation. "It is the providence of God that he has chosen this hour for a campaign," he said one evening in Los Angeles. God was "giving this city one more chance to repent of sin and turn to a believing knowledge of Jesus Christ." He added, "This may be God's last great call!"[6] He would use the basic sermon template to great effect throughout the rest of his career.

The response to his sermons inside the Canvas Cathedral was extraordinary. Crowds packed the tent every night. By the fifth week of the eight-week campaign, a second tent with 9,000 more seats was added. People arrived hours before services were scheduled to begin. Thousands arrived early only to find all

INQUIRERS AND COUNSELORS

Inquirers, those who came forward in response to invitations at rallies, were the most important people at every Graham service. Once they came forward, Graham made sure they understood that only God, not he or the counselors trained by him and his staff, had the power to forgive their sins and change their lives. "You have not come to Billy Graham. . . . I'm just a human being like you. I'm just the messenger. The message you have is from God. You have asked for his forgiveness."[7] Counselors would then lead each individual in a prayer of repentance and personal acceptance of Jesus Christ. Finally, counselors offered advice about finding and joining local churches that matched each person's choice of denomination.

the seats filled. At every service, Graham urged people to make the right decision and come forward. Each night, hundreds did. By the time the Christ for Greater Los Angeles campaign ended on November 30, 1949, an estimated 350,000 people had come to the services and approximately 3,000 had accepted Jesus as their savior.[8]

Much of the success of the campaign was due to publishing tycoon William Randolph Hearst. He was always looking for the next big thing to "puff," or create excitement, so he could sell more newspapers. Noticing Graham's enormous appeal during the Los Angeles campaign, he sent telegrams ordering his editors to "puff Graham."[9] Newspapers all over the country began running stories about the handsome young preacher. Photo stories began appearing in two of the United States's most widely read magazines, *Time* and *Life*. Together, the flood of publicity helped propel Graham into national prominence.

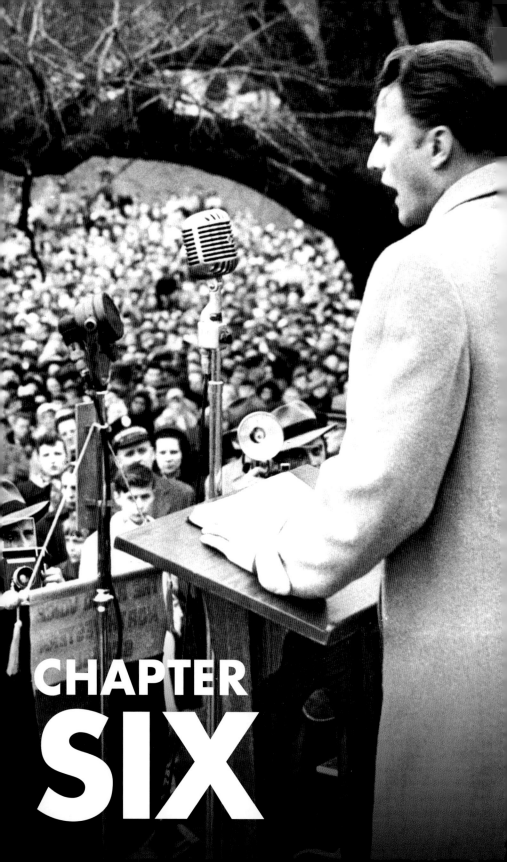

CHAPTER
SIX

HOUR OF DECISION

After Los Angeles, Graham and his team went east to New England. In Boston on New Year's Eve 1949, Graham held a service with little preplanning or publicity. Thousands still showed up, and even bigger crowds flooded to hear him speak the next day. The last meeting of that campaign, at the Boston Garden arena 18 days later, drew more than 25,000 people.[1]

Fame

As a new decade dawned, Graham returned to his home in North Carolina, exhausted and somewhat perplexed. The amazing response of people to his gospel ministry was beyond anything he had ever experienced. But his soaring fame stirred his anxiety. Almost overnight, he became a national figure. He was recognized, and occasionally mobbed, wherever he went. Reporters hounded him for comments on virtually every subject and quoted him as if he were some sort of authority or prophet. All of this attention was overwhelming.

Graham regularly drew large crowds in Boston.

He had not intended to bring praise on himself but to glorify God.

Like many fledgling celebrities, Graham discovered scrutiny by the press could be troublesome. His passionate nature and humble background sometimes caused him to make misstatements and embarrassing errors. Sometimes speculations about the return of Christ got him in trouble. For example, in 1950, he predicted Christ would return within a few years.

Amusing blunders were one thing. Breeches of political etiquette were something else entirely. Graham had said repeatedly he wanted to meet President Harry S. Truman and urge him to establish a national day of prayer in the United States. Truman was reluctant to see the brash young preacher but finally did invite Graham and several members

A GROWING ORGANIZATION

Graham spoke of the sudden growth and success of his ministry in his 1997 book, *Just as I Am: The Autobiography of Billy Graham*:

Overnight we had gone from being a little evangelistic team . . . to what appeared to many to be the hope for national and international revival. Everywhere we turned, someone wanted us to come and do for them what had been done in Los Angeles. What they didn't know however, was that we had not done it. . . . Whatever this could be called and whatever it would become, it was God's doing.[2]

Graham, *second from right*, and friends including Barrows, *second from left*, and Wilson, *right*, pray for Truman outside the White House.

of his ministerial team to meet him in the Oval Office in 1950. Graham did not know presidential visitors were not supposed to tell the press what had happened during their private meetings. Graham talked about the meeting in detail afterward, and he even posed for photographers, kneeling in prayer on the White House lawn. Angry, assuming Graham had used him for publicity, Truman banned him from all future contacts.

Starting an Organization

Embarrassing though that political blunder was, it did not hurt Graham's popularity or his ministry, which continued to grow in 1950. First, he officially founded the BGEA. Other evangelists had received criticism about their salaries and how they used offerings taken at campaigns called crusades. After a 1950 crusade service in Atlanta, Georgia, Graham was photographed smiling broadly, holding large bags stuffed with offering money collected that evening. Newspapers all over the country ran the photo. The implication he had been caught laughing all the way to the bank troubled Graham greatly. Not long after, the BGEA was formed mainly to make sure money would never again become a distraction in his ministry. He wanted to avoid any suspicion or criticism that he was exploiting people. Once the BGEA was formed, all money he collected went directly to the organization, which paid his and his associates' salaries. Graham's first yearly paycheck was $15,000, approximately what a church pastor would be making at the time.[3] His salary rose considerably over the years, and Graham and his growing family lived simply yet comfortably. Given the billions of dollars the

BGEA would eventually earn and spend, few would ever accuse Graham of greed or mishandling funds.

In 1950, the Grahams celebrated the birth of a third daughter, Ruth, as well as the addition of yet another key component to their growing ministry. The latter was the beginning of the radio program *Hour of Decision* on the American Broadcasting Company (ABC) national network of stations. Graham's wife, Ruth, suggested

BGEA AT THE MOVIES

Another significant BGEA media ministry is World Wide Pictures. Established in 1951 as Billy Graham Evangelistic Film Ministry, the venture was a way to document Graham's campaign in Portland, Oregon. Soon, though, Graham and his associates decided to make a Christian western. *Mr. Texas* was low budget and did not use the latest technology. Yet to Graham's amazement, after the premiere showing, 500 people responded to an invitation at the end of the movie to come forward and make a commitment to Christ.[4] Hundreds of films followed, most of them far better technically than the first. Taken together, they demonstrate Graham's early commitment to "spread the gospel by any and all means possible" as the original articles of incorporation of BGEA state.[5]

World Wide Pictures made and distributed a number of notable films. The 1965 film *The Restless Ones*, about sex, drugs, and rock and roll, was BGEA's first movie to appear in commercial theaters. Approximately 4.5 million people viewed it in its first few years.[6] *The Hiding Place* in 1975 starred actress Julie Harris and was based on true events during the Holocaust carried out by the Nazis against the Jews during World War II. *Joni*, released in 1980, was the true story of quadriplegic artist Joni Eareckson Tada.

the title because it perfectly summarized the end goal of each of his messages, calling listeners to a decision for Christ. Each 30-minute show featured religious music wrapped around one of Graham's powerful four-point-formula sermons. After a prayer, Graham would close with a farewell delivered in his Carolina drawl: "And now, until next week, good-bye, and may the Lord bless you real good." *Hour of Decision* became an immediate sensation. Within a few months, an estimated 20 million listeners heard the program on Sunday nights on nearly 1,000 stations in the United States. In 1951, ABC launched its television network and broadcast a visual version of *Hour of Decision* in prime time on Sunday nights. The television show ran for nearly three years.[7] The radio program changed formats several times over the

COUNSELORS

By 1951, most of the parts necessary for the BGEA to conduct large-scale city and region-wide campaigns were in place. The last one was the creation and installation of a standard system for counseling the ever-increasing numbers of inquirers coming forward at crusades. Previously, Graham and his associates, along with a handful of volunteers, worked with people making decisions. After 1952, BGEA workers trained local ministers, who in turn recruited and trained teams of local counselors. This freed BGEA associates to do other things and ensured that guidance stayed in place long after the BGEA team had moved on.

years, with decreasing participation by Graham as time
passed. It went off air in 2014. It continued online,
however, hosted by longtime BGEA associate Cliff
Barrows until he died in 2016.

Religion and Politics

In the dead of winter in 1952, Graham held a five-week
campaign in Washington, DC. When he requested
permission to hold the final meeting of the campaign
on the steps of the Capitol, the request was granted.
Approximately 40,000 people attended the rally, the
first formal religious service ever held on the Capitol
steps.[8] Many in attendance were House and Senate
members, other government officials, and their families.
During that service, Graham called for a national day
of prayer. Soon, the first Thursday of May became the
National Day of Prayer.

Graham's Washington campaign was a landmark for
him in many respects. Mainly, though, it established
him as a leading religious figure in the United States.
It also allowed him to make connections with high
political figures who would later offer opportunities
for his ministry both in the United States and around
the world.

Only two days after Graham called for a national day of prayer,
it was introduced and passed in the House of Representatives.

Graham's travels and lengthy absences from home created difficulties for Ruth and their children. In 1952, the Grahams' fourth child arrived, William Franklin III. Ruth gave all her children a great deal of care and attention, but the children missed their father. Yet Ruth always encouraged her husband's ministry opportunities. She reminded him often that God had called him to evangelism.

In 1953, Graham held rallies in six US cities. The most successful campaign was in Dallas, Texas, at the famed 75,000-seat Cotton Bowl, which was filled to capacity at the final service.[9] At that time, it set a record for the largest evangelistic service ever held in the United States. That was only the beginning. With Graham's ministry at full throttle, he was about to embark on a journey that his younger self would not have imagined in his wildest dreams.

CHAPTER
SEVEN

GRAHAM AND CIVIL RIGHTS

Graham's Chattanooga, Tennessee, campaign of March 1953 would not be particularly memorable, except for an incident that occurred before the first service. It had long been a custom in the South that public events, including religious meetings, were segregated. White people sat in the front rows of a tent or auditorium. African Americans were required to sit in a colored section at the back, often set apart by rope barriers. *Colored* meant races other than white.

Graham had stated previously he objected to racial segregation at meetings he held in the South. However, until Chattanooga, he had never actually done anything about it. The night before the campaign was set to begin, Graham told members of the organizing committee that people should be allowed to sit anywhere they pleased, regardless of skin color. No one listened. When Graham arrived for the service the following day, the ropes were

In the South during the early and mid-1900s, white people enforced segregation in many areas of life.

still in place. Uncharacteristically angry, he ordered ushers to remove them. When they refused, he tore the ropes down himself. When a white usher tried to put them back, Graham told organizers, "Either these ropes stay down, or you can go on and have the revival without me."[1]

Graham's contribution to the civil rights movement is contested. Some people think the stand he took against racial injustice was vitally important. Many others believe Graham did not do nearly enough for the cause and failed miserably to fulfill his obligation as a Christian leader.

Successes and Shortcomings

Graham readily admitted he had embraced the concept of racial equality late in life. Growing up

COME TO THE FRONT

In the early 1940s, while still a student preacher at Wheaton College, Graham was preaching a revival service in the South. At one point, he noticed an African American child who had wandered forward and was playing with a white child toward the front. As a white woman began to guide the black child back to the colored section, Graham appeared and tapped the woman on the shoulder. "You're going the wrong way, Sister," he said. "All the children belong down front so God can smile on them."[2] He took the child's hand and led her forward. That child, recalling the incident as a grown woman some 40 years later, remembered Graham then called for all children, black and white, to come to the front to sit.

in the rural South, he said, "I had adopted the attitudes of that region without much reflection."[3] Only later at Wheaton College did he begin to recognize the struggles African Americans faced.

Through the 1940s and early 1950s, he sometimes did and said things that caused people to suspect him of straddling the fence on the issue of race. During an early crusade in Jackson, Mississippi, for instance, he preached to a segregated crowd. Yet during the sermon, he stated, "There is no scriptural basis for segregation." Soon after, he added, "It may be there are places where [segregation] is desirable to both races, but certainly not in the church."[4] Later, he said he was convinced "church people should be the first to step forward and practice what Christ taught—there is no difference in the sight of God."[5]

Then, the Supreme Court's *Brown v. Board of Education of Topeka* ruling of May 1954 stated segregation in public schools contradicted the US Constitution. Graham never again spoke at a segregated gathering. But neither did Graham participate in any marches or demonstrations protesting racial injustice. He even stated once that he believed Communist agitators inspired such protests in the South. Such comments were not popular with

Three lawyers who fought for the desegregation of public schools in *Brown v. Board of Education* were, *from left to right*, George E. C. Hayes, Thurgood Marshall, and James M. Nabrit.

civil rights leaders such as Dr. Martin Luther King Jr. Throughout the 1950s and 1960s, King and others engaged in a desperate struggle to organize in the face of growing violence against African American protests in Southern cities, including some in Alabama. They needed all the help they could get, but Graham, a leading white religious leader of the time, was unwilling to openly stand with them.

That does not mean he ignored them, however. Graham and King, according to both men's memoirs, were friends. They met on many occasions and exchanged ideas and opinions. King once speculated that his own work for civil rights would not have seen so much success if Graham hadn't also been working at the same time.

According to Graham, King advised him not to become directly involved in marches and protests. Graham said in his autobiography that King told him to keep preaching large crusades because Graham had more influence over white people. Some civil rights leaders believe Graham misunderstood what King said. King was constantly urging white ministers to get more actively involved in the struggle. Despite this, Stephen Miller, history professor and author of a book about Graham's political activities, firmly believes Graham and King both understood each other and their different situations perfectly. Graham, Miller said, "could reach an audience that civil rights activists obviously could not. And on several notable occasions, he made a point of using that sway to link his evangelistic message with racial tolerance."[6]

One such occasion was Graham's 16-week New York City crusade in the summer of 1957. Only a few weeks earlier, President Dwight D. Eisenhower had ordered federal troops to Little Rock, Arkansas. School officials there had refused to obey the law and desegregate the city's schools, and the president needed to make a firm statement. Graham had privately urged Eisenhower to make that move and then publicly supported it. Eisenhower, in turn, asked Graham to see if he could exert any influence he had to help calm rising tensions in the South.

So Graham invited King to deliver the opening prayer at a Madison Square Garden service on July 18. Also, perhaps at King's suggestion, Graham added his first black associate minister, Howard Jones, to his BGEA team.

In 1963, the 16th Street Baptist Church in Birmingham was bombed. The church, whose members were mostly African American, was often the center for civil rights events, and the bombers were thought to have been white supremacists. The blast killed four black girls ages 11 to 14.[7] Graham told fellow evangelicals: "We should have been leading the way to racial justice but we failed. Let's confess it, let's admit it, and let's do something about it."[8]

Protests and demonstrations grew angrier and more violent. Civil rights leaders increasingly disassociated themselves from Graham and BGEA activities. Graham gradually began to realize his attempts to act as the

United States's racial mediator were probably futile. His original mission, winning souls for Christ, was the only thing that could change hatred and racism. It was time to rededicate himself to his original calling.

THE NEO-EVANGELICALISM MOVEMENT

Graham's stance on race was one aspect of his gradual shift away from traditional fundamentalists such as Mordecai Ham and Bob Jones Sr. and toward a more moderate brand of Christianity known as neo-evangelicalism, or new evangelicalism. Those associated with the new movement, including Graham, held fast to many of the most treasured aspects of Protestant fundamentalism. Among them were the divinity of Jesus Christ (meaning Jesus was God); the belief that the Bible is God's sacred word to humankind; the need for all people to put their faith in Jesus Christ; and an emphasis on spreading the gospel through evangelism. But neo-evangelists rejected the idea that Christianity had to be practiced inside a hard shell that excluded, rather than embraced, alternative ideas, denominations, and cultural and racial differences. Graham's ecumenism, especially his eagerness to embrace all denominations, including Catholics, during his large-scale crusades beginning in the 1950s, illustrates this most clearly. In 1956, Graham launched a new magazine, *Christianity Today*, to publish and spread his neo-evangelistic viewpoint. Many scholars believe Graham's leadership at World Congress on Evangelism conferences in Berlin, Germany, in 1966 and Lausanne, Switzerland, in 1974 began the spread of this new ecumenical movement worldwide.

CHAPTER
EIGHT

INTERNATIONAL MINISTRIES

B y the mid-1950s, Graham was convinced his call to preach the gospel of Jesus Christ was not limited to the United States. However, his first attempt to export large-scale evangelism did not get off to a promising start. When he announced he would stage a campaign in the United Kingdom in 1954, many religious leaders there were not enthused. Neither was the notoriously cynical London, United Kingdom, press. People told Graham the British were reserved and unemotional by nature, particularly about religion. Some people in the United Kingdom remembered Graham's visit nearly a decade earlier during his YFC ministry. Some thought his brand of preaching then was overly theatrical and confrontational, and they assumed he had not changed. The British newspapers referred to "silly Billy" and the imminent arrival of his "American hot gospel circus."[1]

When Graham arrived in London, he held a press conference with more than 100 reporters.

GOD SAVE THE QUEEN

Before he left the United Kingdom, Graham received an invitation to preach at a private chapel service for Queen Elizabeth II and the royal family. Whether he also presented a Christian invitation to the royal family at the close of his sermon is not known. Following strict custom, Graham shared no details of his visit. Afterward, he lunched with the Queen and the Queen Mother at Windsor Castle in Berkshire County west of London. Elizabeth II and Graham remained mutual admirers for the rest of his life.

The United Kingdom campaign began in London at Harringay Arena. To Graham's relief, people packed the auditorium on the first night. He did note, however, that many of them appeared to be members of the media. News stories the next day reported Graham had spoken much too quickly and too loudly and that many in the audience had trouble understanding his odd American accent. Yet 200 young people had come forward in response to Graham's invitation, a response that puzzled some observers.[2] The press expressed surprise at the sincerity and depth of Graham's message and especially the preacher's humble manner.

People from all over the United Kingdom began flocking to London for the services. But the arena only held approximately 12,000 people.[3] Many were turned away night after night without hearing the gospel.

People who responded to Graham's invitation at Harringay Arena gathered around the podium.

An ABC engineer, there to record Graham's sermons for *Hour of Decision*, offered a solution. He worked with British telephone companies to send an audio feed from the arena through existing phone lines to all parts of the United Kingdom. Receivers and loudspeakers were set up in more than 430 churches and other places all across England, Ireland, Scotland, and Wales.[4] Many radio stations broadcast the transmission, too. The final service of the London campaign was held at Wembley Stadium in the pouring rain. An estimated 120,000 packed the venue.[5] Graham left the United Kingdom and toured western Europe with campaigns in eight large cities. He returned to the United Kingdom for a campaign in Scotland followed by another week in London with meetings every night.

Family Time

Throughout the 1950s, Graham interspersed large crusades in the United States between trips to India, Japan, and Korea. After each exhausting trek, he hurried home to rest and prepare for the next crusade. By then, Graham had achieved such a level of fame and notoriety that people were constantly knocking on the door, asking for autographs, and gazing in through windows. It was time to find a less public place to live and raise the children.

The answer was a mountaintop retreat at Little Piney Cove, surrounded by 150 wooded acres (60 ha) overlooking Montreat.[6] While Graham was away, Ruth arranged the financing and designed and directed the building of the sprawling, rustic house. By 1956, the finished result was a one-of-a-kind homestead. There

Ruth and children enthusiastically welcomed Graham when he returned home from his travels. Ruth traveled with him whenever she could.

was plenty of room for their last child, Nelson, who was born in 1958.

Graham could not have performed the work he did without Ruth's love and support. Her deep knowledge of the Bible was a resource her husband regularly consulted for advice and sermon illustrations. She did not hesitate to disagree when she felt it was warranted. When, for instance, Graham decided to join the Baptist church, Ruth declined to give up her own Presbyterian membership, which she retained throughout her life. It was not the only thing they disagreed about, but the relationship remained loving.

Graham's children missed their father while he was gone, but they assumed that was what all dads did. Graham's eldest daughter Virginia, known as Gigi, did not consider the toll those long absences had on her father himself until one day when Graham disciplined her for something she had done. She ran to her room and slammed the door. Soon after, she heard his angry footsteps approaching. He came into her room, sat her down, and scolded her. Stung, she yelled, "Some dad you are! You go away and leave us alone all the time!"[7] Immediately, she saw her father's eyes fill with tears. She realized for the first time the sacrifice he was making leaving them behind to go minister to others. She also noticed that after that day, her father did not seem to discipline the children quite so much.

Reaching the World

Despite the personal sacrifices, the work Graham felt compelled to do was often exhilarating. In 1959 in Australia and New Zealand, Graham experienced one of the most extraordinary responses to the gospel that he, and possibly anyone else, had ever witnessed. During that campaign, approximately 50 percent of Australia's ten million people heard Graham preach, either in person or on the radio or television. Documented decisions after those events were estimated at approximately 130,000.[8]

Graham's world travels continued over the next three decades through Africa, the Middle East, and South America. Many times, Graham had to deal with strong anti-American feelings and demonstrations in those places, the result of political entanglements and policies over which he had no control. Sometimes he faced criticism at home as well, particularly for his failure to speak out against harsh, unjust, or nondemocratic leaders and governments of countries he visited. This was especially true of Communist nations.

In 1982, Graham visited the Soviet Union, which would

SEOUL WINNER

Nothing illustrates Graham's success at foreign evangelism better than his 1973 evangelistic campaign in South Korea. In the nation's capital of Seoul, between May 30 and June 3, Graham preached to an estimated 3.2 million people.[9] More than one million people traveled from all over South Korea to attend the final service held on a mile-long airstrip on Yeouido Island in the middle of the Han River. According to BGEA records, some 75,000 inquirers made decisions for Christ during that campaign, the largest Graham ever conducted. Graham biographer William Martin has called the final Yeouido service "almost certainly the largest public religious gathering in history."[10]

later split into multiple countries, the largest of which is Russia. During the Cold War (1947–1962), there was extreme tension between the Communist Soviet Union and the democratic United States over which system of government was better. Graham agreed to preach only the gospel while in the Soviet Union and make no political statements. During that trip, Graham met with a group of Soviet Christians who had taken refuge in the American embassy in Siberia. Known as the Siberian Seven, they were seeking political asylum, but the Soviet government had forbidden them from leaving the country. Graham met and prayed with

"FRIEND OF ISRAEL"

Graham had wanted to travel to Israel, where Jesus Christ was born and Christianity began, for years. In 1960, he finally received a wary invitation from Israeli religious and political leaders. The country is primarily Jewish. The government warned him to make no attempt to convert Jews to Christianity. Jerusalem newspapers were particularly critical, given the long anti-Semitic history of fundamentalist Protestant preachers. Graham managed to charm his potential critics and still get his message across. During an interview in Jerusalem, he said he wanted to thank Israel "for being the nation through which Jesus was brought to this earth in the divine plan of God. And I want to thank you as one who has given my life to a Jew, who living upon this earth, claimed to be God."[11] Later, Israeli president Golda Meir gave Graham a Christian Bible. She signed it with the inscription, "To a great teacher in all the important matters to humanity and a dear friend of Israel."[12]

them, but, keeping his word, made no critical remarks about the Soviets. In fact, despite the obvious distress of the Siberian Seven, Graham said after his trip that he "had not personally seen any evidence of religious persecution."[13]

His statements set off a firestorm of criticism in the United States. He was accused of being a traitor and fool for allowing the Soviets to use him for propaganda. Walter Smyth, a member of Graham's BGEA staff, later said, "Of course [the Soviets] are using us. But we are using them as well, to get the gospel out to their people."[14] Graham added later that if he had gone back on his word and made political statements, the Soviets never would have let him come back as they did in 1984 and 1988. By not antagonizing his hosts and continuing to plant the seeds of Christianity, Graham believed he was able to quietly chip away at the foundations of power in the Soviet Union.

CHAPTER
NINE

ADVISING PRESIDENTS

L ittle brought Graham more spiritual pain than his fascination with politics and power, and especially his friendships and associations with US presidents. Biographers and historians such as David Aikman and William Martin generally agree that most presidents, to some degree, used Graham's popular appeal to enhance their own public images. In addition, according to Aikman, Graham's willingness to be used might well have diluted the power of his Christian message during the final decades of his ministry.

Graham's first encounter with an American president, when he met Harry S. Truman, did not go well. Besides talking about his first visit to the Oval Office with the press, he also offered his opinion that the president was mishandling the Korean War (1950–1953). Graham's subsequent ban from the

Graham advised many presidents, including Lyndon B. Johnson.

Truman White House was a learning experience for him.

Graham's relationship with the next president, Dwight D. Eisenhower, was much friendlier. Graham greatly admired General Eisenhower, as did most of the nation after World War II. Graham urged him to run in the 1952 presidential election. Eisenhower asked Graham for advice, both religious and political. After Eisenhower's declining health forced him to leave politics, Graham ministered to the former president as pastor and friend. That relationship continued until Eisenhower's death in 1968. Graham continued playing the role of occasional adviser over the next 50 years.

GRAHAM'S INFLUENCE ON EISENHOWER

Eisenhower specifically asked for Graham's input while he was composing his address for the presidential inauguration. The address had a religious theme. Graham also suggested that Eisenhower join a Washington, DC, church, which the president did. Writer David Aikman believes Eisenhower's 1955 signing of a measure to put "in God We Trust" on US money can also be directly traced to Graham's spiritual influence. The following year, Eisenhower also officially made those words the national motto, replacing the Latin phrase *E pluribus Unum.*

Adviser to Presidents

Graham's connection with Democrat John F. Kennedy

was not particularly close. During the 1960 presidential campaign, Graham supported Kennedy's opponent, Republican Richard Nixon, though not vocally and not while preaching. Still, he declined to join a host of other Protestant ministers who furiously rallied against Kennedy because of his Catholic faith. Graham even promised Kennedy if he won the election, Graham would support him wholeheartedly thereafter. Graham kept his word, but they never got the chance to form any sort of relationship before Kennedy's assassination in 1963.

One of the closest connections Graham ever had with a sitting president was with Lyndon B. Johnson, who became president upon Kennedy's death. Though their personalities were quite different, Johnson and Graham hit it off from the start. Graham, sometimes with Ruth, spent many nights at Johnson's Texas ranch and at the White House. Graham served as Johnson's spiritual counselor and supported him politically.

Vietnam War

The Vietnam War (1954–1975) was raging during Johnson's presidency. Communist North Vietnam and its allies in South Vietnam fought against the

Johnson often sought out Graham when he needed spiritual support.

government of South Vietnam and the United States.
North Vietnam wanted Communism to govern the
country. South Vietnam and the United States did not
want Communism to spread. US military involvement
in the Vietnam War reached its peak between 1965 and
1968. During that period, the war became increasingly
unpopular among Americans. A mostly youth-led
peace movement in the United States opposed the war
through chaotic and sometimes violent demonstrations.

Protesters argued that civilians, not enemy fighters, were the primary victims of US air strikes.

Graham visited Vietnam in 1966 and found the situation worse than he expected. He could see no evidence that the US military's massive bombings and buildup of troops there were making any real impact on shortening the war. However, Johnson was already distraught over his inability to end the war. So Graham publicly continued to echo and support the Johnson administration's assertion that the war was going well and was still winnable. The war ended with the withdrawal of US forces in 1973 and the unification of Vietnam under Communist control two years later. More than three million people, including 58,000 Americans, died in the conflict.[1]

After Johnson left office in 1969 and until his death in 1973, Graham served as presidential pastor. He and Johnson had lengthy discussions about salvation and the afterlife, and at Johnson's request, Graham preached an evangelistic message at Johnson's graveside service.

Graham and Nixon

Nixon became president after Johnson. The relationship between Graham and Nixon was extraordinary in many ways. As writer William Martin has summarized it, no American president has "ever made such a conscious, calculating use of religion as a political instrument as did [Nixon with Graham]."[2] Nixon promoted Graham's image, which Nixon specifically exploited to give a religious cast to his largely secular and ultimately criminal presidency. Meanwhile, Graham failed to recognize he was being used in this way. According to biographer David Aikman, Graham's failure to detect Nixon's character flaws exposed two of Graham's own principal weaknesses—his desire to be liked and his inability to see deception or malice in others.

For Graham, his relationship with Nixon was one of genuine friendship and admiration. He once even described the president as "every inch a Christian gentleman."[3] Yet while Graham often led prayer and Bible studies at the White House, insiders said Nixon never prayed or actively participated. Graham assumed this had something to do with the fact that Nixon was a Quaker, a form of Christianity that does not stress sermons or public prayer but rather the development of one's own faith. What Graham did not know was Nixon had deep personal doubts about many fundamentalist principles of the Christian faith, including the literal

Graham was a vocal supporter of Nixon, *right*, during the 1968 presidential campaign.

truth of the Bible. Though they discussed religious matters many times, Nixon never revealed his doubts to Graham. Graham recalled, years later, that Nixon had always assured him he believed the Bible cover to cover.

Nixon's lack of outward religious feeling never bothered Graham as much as loud, sometimes vulgar protests against Nixon. Many believed Nixon had failed to honorably end the war in Vietnam.

One such demonstration erupted on Billy Graham Day in Charlotte on October 15, 1971. It was a special celebration for the city to honor local hero Graham. The day turned into a noisy, chaotic protest against the president when Nixon showed up to speak. Graham was shocked.

When reports about Nixon's involvement in wiretapping and other criminal activities at the

HAUNTING REMINDERS

Graham's close association with Nixon came back to haunt him once again in 2002 when a batch of tapes recorded in the White House in 1972 were released to the public. One of them contained a conversation between the president and Graham during which the preacher had made several strongly anti-Semitic, or anti-Jewish, remarks. Deeply embarrassed and repentant, Graham begged people to accept his many pro-Jewish actions and words since 1972 as representative of his true feelings rather than a few remarks he called careless. His apologies were largely accepted, though the remarks had made irreparable damage for some.

The anti-Jewish sentiments Graham expressed, whether his true feelings or not, were not new. In fact, many early fundamentalists considered Jews evil and a danger to Christianity. Mordecai Ham preached anti-Semitism along with the gospel during revival meetings. He sometimes even called out local Jewish merchants by name and urged Christians to avoid dealing with them. Graham did not actively follow Ham's example in regards to anti-Semitism. Still, columnist Dennis Roddy could not help wondering after the Nixon debacle if, perhaps, "a bit of Mordecai Ham found its way into Graham's marrow."[4]

Democratic Party's Watergate Building headquarters began to come out, Graham refused to believe them at first. He continued to support the president even as evidence mounted, choosing to assume, as Aiken has suggested, the role of a supportive pastor.

Nixon had a desperate desire to be reelected in 1972 and remain in power. So he ordered or knowingly allowed dozens of staff members, advisers, and subordinates to perform illegal and deceptive activities. Their list of crimes included spying, wiretapping, bribery, robbery, threats, and conspiracy. All of it was part of a master plan orchestrated by Nixon and his aides. As the scheme unraveled, the president involved many high-ranking officials in order to shield his unconstitutional activities. Graham was devastated when Nixon resigned in August 1974. But Graham's worst suffering came later, when transcripts, or written copies, of secret tape recordings of Nixon's White House conversations emerged. They proved the full extent of Nixon's guilt in masterminding the elaborate web of illegal schemes and deceptions that became known as the Watergate Scandal.

As Graham read the transcripts detailing Nixon's activities, he became physically ill and wept bitterly.

In the days that followed, he isolated himself to reflect and pray. He had trouble sleeping. He later said of Nixon: "I think I always thought a great deal more of him than he thought of me."[5]

The thing that upset Graham most about the revelations in the transcripts was Nixon's liberal use of profanity. The words represented a stunning level of deception. Graham could not remember one time in all the years he had known Nixon when he ever heard Nixon use such language.

Back to Work

Within a few weeks, Graham returned to public life, seemingly recovered and eager to get back to work preaching the gospel. The following April, Graham was invited to deliver the opening prayer for a session of Congress. "Forgive us if we have compromised our ideals," he prayed.[6] Graham confided later to a convicted Watergate conspirator, Charles Colson, that he made

HIGH HONORS

Calling Graham "one of the most inspirational spiritual leaders of the twentieth century," President Reagan presented Graham with the Presidential Medal of Freedom, the nation's highest nonmilitary award, in 1983.[7] Graham also received the Congressional Gold Medal, the highest honor Congress can bestow on a private citizen, in 1996.

a mistake in becoming friends with Nixon. "Billy told me," Colson said, "he would never make the mistake again of getting that close to someone in office."[8]

Graham's mistakes did not stop him from venturing back to the White House whenever he was invited. He did just that in 1975, barely six months after his ordeal with Nixon, when President Gerald R. Ford invited him. Afterward, Graham told reporters they had read the Bible together and prayed. But although presidents and their wives were friendly, the relationship between president and presidential pastor never became as close as it had been during the Nixon years.

CHAPTER
TEN

FINISHING THE COURSE

D an Rather and his roommate, both young journalism students, attended a Graham service in Houston, Texas, in the 1950s. They were eager to prove that Graham was a fraud and his massive crusade machine was nothing but a moneymaking scheme. But at the vast stadium venue, as they watched and listened, they began to change their minds. By the end of Graham's fiery sermon, Rather wrote, "It was all we could do to hold each other back" from responding with hundreds of others to Graham's poignant call to repentance. "Our cynicism had just completely melted away."[1]

As Rather and millions of others over the years learned, "there was a kind of magic in a Billy Graham Crusade at that time" that was as hard to resist as it was to fully explain.[2] Throughout the latter half of the 1900s and into the 2000s, Graham and his BGEA

Many skeptics accepted Graham's invitation to accept Jesus as their savior.

GRAHAM'S VIEWS ON HOMOSEXUALITY

Graham largely agreed with and preached the traditional principle that gay and lesbian relationships are a sin and that gay marriage should be illegal. In 1993, he said during a crusade sermon he thought AIDS might represent "a judgment of God" against gay and lesbian relationships. He later retracted that remark, saying, "I don't believe that, and I don't know why I said it."[4] Yet, in 2012, Graham ran full-page ads supporting an amendment to the North Carolina state constitution banning same-sex marriage. For the most part after that, however, Graham stuck to a position that he did not want to talk about the political issues important to other evangelical conservatives, such as abortion or homosexuality. That did not appease many thousands who never forgave Graham for what they saw as a half-century crusade against LGBTQ people.

team continued to confront multitudes with the gospel message, to plead for them to make decisions for Christ, because they might not get another chance.

Easing Up

Graham gradually drifted away from the brand of fundamentalist Christianity he embraced when he was first converted. In a 1978 *McCall's* magazine article, Graham made the startling admission he had actually changed his mind about how salvation itself works. "I believe that there are other ways of recognizing the existence of God," he said. "Through nature, for instance, and plenty of other opportunities, therefore, of saying 'yes' to God."[3] In 1993, in a *Time* magazine interview,

Graham said his idea of Hell had changed, as well. "Hell," he said, simply "means separation from God. . . . When it comes to literal fire, I don't preach it because I'm not sure about it."[5]

What he was sure about, he said at age 87, was that "the Lord has just gradually changed me." He told an interviewer, "I guess I became more mellow and more forgiving and more loving." He said his "overwhelming message is the grace and the love and the mercy of God. And that's what I emphasize now."[6]

Inspiration to Change

One step in reaching that point was his visit to the site of the former Nazi death camp at Auschwitz, Poland, in 1978. The Nazi political party of Germany killed many Jews and people with disabilities during World War II. After his visit, Graham said he realized "peace was a moral issue and not just a political issue, and we are to be instruments of [God's] peace whenever possible."[7] He began to speak more frequently and emphatically against war and terrorism and urged evangelicals worldwide to unite to eliminate nuclear and biological weapons. Thus, in his later years, Graham shifted further away from preaching a God of uncompromising wrath and judgment and toward preaching a God of infinite love, compassion, and peace.

This shift, according to Aikman, also placed him in the ideal position to assume the final role of his life—that of national consoler. Graham fulfilled that role in 1995 after a domestic terrorist bombed a federal building in Oklahoma City, Oklahoma. In the bombing, 168 people were killed and some 800 were injured.[8]

FRANKLIN AND ANNE

Graham's son Franklin became president of the BGEA in 2001. An ordained minister, Franklin has also been president of Samaritan's Purse since 1979. The organization provides Christian evangelism and training along with disaster relief and humane assistance to people in more than 100 countries around the world. In his 1995 autobiography, *Rebel With a Cause*, Franklin described his wild youth, conversion, and eventual call to preach the gospel. At first, Franklin was as reluctant to accept the call to preach. He knew he would always be compared to his father, and he felt certain he could never measure up. He finally gave in, and since then he has preached around the world. He conducts what he likes to call festivals, choosing a different name from that of his father's campaigns. However, his purpose is still the same. "I just want to be faithful to the same message that he's been faithful to, and that's the preaching of the gospel," he said.[9]

Graham's daughter Anne Graham Lotz is also influential. In the late 1980s, Lotz established AnGeL ministries, through which she offered Just Give Me Jesus revivals, which still run today. After hearing her speak, her father once called her "the best preacher in the family."[10] Lotz is also a best-selling and award-winning author of 11 books.[11]

At a memorial service a few days later, Graham urged a grieving crowd to embrace God's enduring love and the hope of eternal life. After the September 11, 2001, terrorist attacks on the World Trade Center in New York, Graham was once again called upon to console a grieving nation. He said he did not know how or why God could allow for such tragedy and suffering. But he assured everyone, as he had throughout his long career, of his belief that faith and forgiveness were still the surest path to personal and national healing.

Legacy

During Graham's active ministry, which lasted some 66 years, he preached to more than 210 million people in all 50 of the United States as well as in 185 nations around the world. More than three million people made decisions for Christ during that time.[12] It is impossible to know the number of lives Graham changed while reading his books, articles, and newspaper columns, listening to his *Hour of Decision* radio program, or watching his movies and telecasts of his crusades. One biographer has noted that during Graham's lifetime, he was almost certainly seen and heard by more people than any other person in history.

GRAHAM'S FAR-REACHING IMPACT[13]

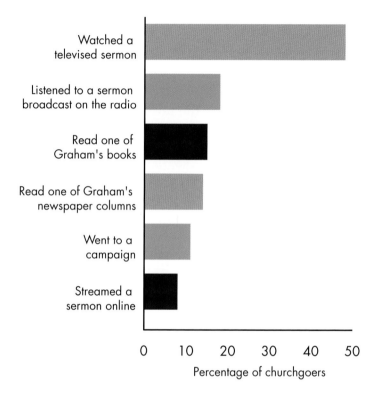

	Percentage of churchgoers
Watched a televised sermon	
Listened to a sermon broadcast on the radio	
Read one of Graham's books	
Read one of Graham's newspaper columns	
Went to a campaign	
Streamed a sermon online	

0   10   20   30   40   50
Percentage of churchgoers

In early 2018, a study revealed how Graham's ministries reached many Protestant and nondenominational American churchgoers.

During his active ministry, Graham, more than any other individual, defined and shaped the evangelical Christian movement worldwide. He pushed Christianity forward into a more inclusive era. Without Graham, "we'd be living in a different world," according to Randall Balmer, chair of the religion department at

Dartmouth College. "Evangelicalism today would have virtually no political or cultural relevance whatsoever."[14] Balmer and others assert the powerful political Christian Right exists today mainly because Graham proved American politics and religion could coexist.

Graham's influence extended far beyond the United States. His evolving vision of Christianity led him to call Christian leaders of many different nations and denominations together under one banner. Between 1966 and 1986, Graham and his BGEA associates sponsored meetings attended by thousands of church leaders from around the world. Evangelists focused on ways to spread the gospel around the world and received training. Those gatherings inspired and set in motion people and programs that are still running today. Because of these meetings, a *Newsweek* magazine article called Graham "one of the most formidable figures in the 2,000-year story of Christian evangelism."[15]

Yet most of the time, by his own admission, Graham did not feel formidable. Quite often, he felt anxious, weak, and ill. He felt exhausted from running around the world, preaching sermon after sermon. The loneliness of the road and the loss of privacy at home sometimes seemed unbearable. There were times when it seemed he was almost sorry he had taken on the task. He said, "I did not ask for this assignment that was pressed on me by a sovereign God." He once even admitted, "Many times I wish the Lord would just take me, because I get so weighted down with the sins of the world, for which I have a constant revulsion."[16] Yet his greatest fear was always that God would someday find him unworthy and make him stop preaching.

God did not force him to stop, but age and illness did. On June 27, 2005, he preached his last official sermon in New York City. At age 86, white hair flowing, stooped and feeble, Graham had to be helped to the podium by his son, Franklin. Once there, he preached for 20 minutes. During his sermon, he told the audience of some 90,000 that he knew it would not be long before he went to

LYING IN STATE

In keeping with his humble beginnings, Graham was buried in a simple pine coffin. The casket, handmade by inmates at the Louisiana State Penitentiary at Angola, was identical to the one in which his wife, Ruth, was laid to rest in 2007. Graham's casket lay in honor in the US Capitol rotunda for several days. Historically only 33 Americans had ever been given that honor. Graham was the fourth private citizen to receive it. Not everyone agreed that Graham deserved such an honor. Some thought honoring a Christian religious leader in this way crossed the line between church and state, a division America's Founding Fathers struggled hard to establish.

Heaven and that he was ready. Then, in his characteristic style, he asked, "Are you prepared? Have you opened your heart to Jesus? Have you repented of your sins?"[17]

Graham died on February 21, 2018, at his home in Montreat, a place that had been his retreat and refuge for many years. He was 99 years old. His final resting place is a grave next to his wife in the memorial garden at the Billy Graham Library in Charlotte. More than 2,000 invited guests attended his funeral.[18] Attendees and speakers included President Donald Trump, Vice President Mike Pence, several governors, and dozens of senators, religious leaders, celebrities, and Graham's family and friends. There were many recollections of his unique and extraordinary life and comments about the meaning of his death. But years earlier, Graham had already delivered his own eulogy, a speech in honor of a person who has died. In a close paraphrase of words spoken by his hero, 1800s revivalist Dwight L. Moody, Graham said:

> Someday you will read or hear that Billy Graham is dead. Don't you believe a word of it. I shall be more alive than I am now. I will just have changed my address. I will have gone into the presence of God.[19]

TIMELINE

1918
On November 7, William Franklin Graham Jr. is born.

1934
On November 1, Graham makes a decision to commit his life to Jesus Christ at a revival meeting.

1936
Graham graduates from high school and sells Fuller brushes door-to-door.

1937
Graham preaches his first official sermon in the spring while still a student at Florida Bible Institute.

1939
Graham is ordained as a Baptist minister.

1943
Graham graduates from Wheaton College and marries Ruth Bell.

1944

On May 27, Graham preaches at the Chicagoland Youth for Christ rally, the beginning of his nearly decade-long association with the organization.

1945

Graham's first child, Virginia, is born, followed by Anne (1948), Ruth (1950), Franklin (1952), and Nelson (1958).

1948

Graham becomes president of Northwestern Schools.

1949

Graham conducts a series of evangelistic meetings called Christ for Greater Los Angeles, which launches him to national prominence.

1950

Graham founds the Billy Graham Evangelistic Association and begins his *Hour of Decision* radio broadcasts.

TIMELINE

1952

Graham preaches on the steps of the Capitol building in Washington, DC. He suggests establishing a national day of prayer. President Harry S. Truman signs the National Day of Prayer into law.

1953

In March at his Chattanooga, Tennessee, campaign, Graham takes down the ropes separating seating for white people and African Americans.

1954

Graham conducts his London rallies and meets Queen Elizabeth II.

1956

Graham establishes the magazine *Christianity Today*.

1957

BGEA stages a massive 16-week campaign in New York City.

1959
BGEA's Australia campaign sparks a massive revival.

1983
President Ronald Reagan presents Graham
with the Presidential Medal of Freedom.

2001
Graham's son Franklin becomes president of the BGEA.

2005
On June 27, 2005, Graham preaches at the
closing of his final campaign in New York City.

2018
On February 21, Graham dies at age 99 in
his home in Montreat, North Carolina.

ESSENTIAL FACTS

Date of Birth
November 7, 1918

Place of Birth
Family's farm near Charlotte, North Carolina

Parents
William and Morrow Graham

Education
Florida Bible Institute (now Trinity College), ThB in theology (1940); Wheaton College, BA in anthropology (1943)

Marriage
Ruth Bell (1943)

Children
Virginia (Gigi), Anne, Ruth, William Franklin, Nelson (Ned)

Career Highlights
Graham was Charter Vice President for Youth for Christ International from 1945 to 1950 and president of Northwestern Schools from 1948 through 1952. Graham founded the Billy Graham Evangelistic Association in 1950. That same year, Graham started the weekly *Hour of Decision* radio program. Graham held many noteworthy

BGEA campaigns. Between 1940 and 2005, Graham preached to some 215 million people in more than 185 countries. He met with every US president from Harry S. Truman to Barack Obama. He published 33 books, and he received the Presidential Medal of Freedom in 1983.

Societal Contributions

Billy Graham was a major figure in American religious and popular culture from the 1950s until his death in 2018. The BGEA carried out mass evangelism on a global scale. Graham's role as pastor to presidents was historic. Graham's work helped create today's political Christian Right. He was certain he had the simple solution to life's most difficult problems. His sharing of that solution changed many lives.

Conflicts

Some protested Graham's support of ecumenism. Some thought Graham didn't do enough for civil rights. Graham faced hardships when he realized Nixon had deceived him.

Quote

"Everywhere we turned, someone wanted us to come and do for them what we'd done in Los Angeles. What they didn't know however, was that we had not done it. . . . Whatever this could be called and whatever it would become, it was God's doing."

—*Billy Graham, recalling the growth of his ministry in his book* Just as I Am: The Autobiography of Billy Graham

GLOSSARY

asylum
Protection given by a country to someone who has left his or her country as a political refugee.

catechism
A collection of questions and answers that are used to teach people about the Christian religion.

console
To give encouragement or comfort to lessen someone's grief, sorrow, or disappointment.

convert
To adopt a new religion as one's own.

denomination
A group within a religion that follows somewhat different teachings and practices than other groups within that same religion.

evangelist
One who preaches the gospel, particularly a traveling revivalist.

fanatic
A person who is carried away beyond reason by his or her feelings or beliefs, usually toward a controversial matter.

formidable
Having awesome strength, force, or power.

fundamentalist
Characterized by a strict belief that the Bible is written without error and should be interpreted literally, and belief in the divinity of Jesus Christ as the Son of God.

hymn
A song of praise, celebration, or worship.

manifesto
A public declaration of opinion.

ordained
To have been officially recognized or appointed for a specific duty or task, such as a minister.

repent
To feel sorrow about one's sins, try to quit sinning, and live a right life.

segregation
The practice of separating groups of people based on race, gender, ethnicity, or other factors.

sovereign
Possessing ultimate power.

white supremacist
Someone who believes that white people are superior to all other races.

ADDITIONAL RESOURCES

Selected Bibliography

Aikman, David. *Billy Graham: His Life and Influence*. Nashville, TN: Thomas Nelson, 2007. Print.

Frady, Marshall. *Billy Graham: A Parable of American Righteousness*. Boston: Little, Brown, 1979. Print.

Graham, Billy. *Just as I Am: The Autobiography of Billy Graham*. Revised and updated 10th anniversary ed. Grand Rapids, MI: HarperOne, 2007. Print.

Martin, William. *A Prophet With Honor: The Billy Graham Story*. Updated ed. Grand Rapids, MI: Zondervan, 2018. Print.

Further Readings

Asselin, Kristine Carlson. *Martin Luther King Jr.: Civil Rights Leader*. Minneapolis: Abdo, 2014. Print.

Bodden, Valerie. *Understanding Christianity*. Minneapolis: Abdo, 2019. Print.

Capek, Michael. *Civil Rights Movement*. Minneapolis: Abdo, 2014. Print.

Online Resources

To learn more about Billy Graham, visit **abdobooklinks.com**. These links are routinely monitored and updated to provide the most current information available.

More Information

For more information on this subject, contact or visit the following organizations:

Billy Graham Center Museum
501 College Avenue
Wheaton, IL 60187
630-752-5000
wheaton.edu/about-wheaton/museum-and-collections/billy-graham-center-museum/slideshow
The Billy Graham Center Museum, located on the campus of Wheaton College, features a visual overview of the history of Christian evangelism and its influence on American society.

Billy Graham Library
4330 Westmont Drive
Charlotte, NC 28217
704-401-3200
billygrahamlibrary.org
This barn-shaped building is only miles from where Graham grew up. The library holds exhibits about Graham's life and work.

SOURCE NOTES

Chapter 1. "Just as I Am"

1. Billy Graham. *Just as I Am: The Autobiography of Billy Graham.* Large print ed. San Francisco: HarperSanFrancisco, 1997. Print. 29.

2. Marshall Frady. *Billy Graham: A Parable of American Righteousness.* Boston: Little, Brown, 1979. Print. 83.

3. Graham, *Just as I Am,* 39.

4. Frady, *Billy Graham,* 84.

5. Graham, *Just as I Am,* 42.

6. Graham, *Just as I Am,* 41.

7. "Just as I Am, Without One Plea," *HymnTime.com.* HymnTime.com, 2018. Web. 14 June 2018.

8. Graham, *Just as I Am,* 43.

9. Graham, *Just as I Am,* 43.

10. "Profile: William (Billy) F. Graham, Jr." *Billy Graham Evangelistic Association.* BGEA, 2018. Web. 14 June 2018.

Chapter 2. Billy Frank

1. Marshall Frady. *Billy Graham: A Parable of American Righteousness.* Boston: Little, Brown, 1979. Print. 79.

2. David Aikman. *Billy Graham: His Life and Influence.* Nashville: Thomas Nelson, 2007. Print. 26.

3. Frady, *Billy Graham,* 70.

4. Billy Graham. *Just as I Am: The Autobiography of Billy Graham.* Large print ed. San Francisco: HarperSanFrancisco, 1997. Print. 46.

5. William Martin. *A Prophet with Honor: The Billy Graham Story.* Updated ed. Grand Rapids, MI: Zondervan, 2018. Print. 69.

6. Frady, *Billy Graham,* 94.

7. Frady, *Billy Graham,* 93.

Chapter 3. "You've Got Me"

1. Marshall Frady. *Billy Graham: A Parable of American Righteousness.* Boston: Little, Brown, 1979. Print. 105.

2. Billy Graham. *Just as I Am: The Autobiography of Billy Graham.* Large print ed. San Francisco: HarperSanFrancisco, 1997. Print. 77.

3. William Martin. *A Prophet with Honor: The Billy Graham Story.* Updated ed. Grand Rapids, MI: Zondervan, 2018. Print. 77.

4. Graham, *Just as I Am,* 78.

5. Frady, *Billy Graham,* 133.

6. David Aikman. *Billy Graham: His Life and Influence.* Nashville: Thomas Nelson, 2007. Print. 41.

7. Martin, *A Prophet with Honor,* 78.

8. Aikman, *Billy Graham,* 280.

9. Martin, *A Prophet with Honor,* 85.

Chapter 4. Youth for Christ

1. William Martin. *A Prophet with Honor: The Billy Graham Story*. Updated ed. Grand Rapids, MI: Zondervan, 2018. Print. 88–89.

2. Martin, *A Prophet with Honor*, 93.

3. Billy Graham. *Just as I Am: The Autobiography of Billy Graham*. Large print ed. San Francisco: HarperSanFrancisco, 1997. Print. 88.

4. "Geared to the Times, Anchored to the Rock." *Youth for Christ International*. YFC, 2018. Web. 22 June 2018.

5. Martin, *A Prophet with Honor*, 98.

6. Martin, *A Prophet with Honor*, 100.

7. Graham, *Just as I Am*, 173.

8. David Aikman. *Billy Graham: His Life and Influence*. Nashville: Thomas Nelson, 2007. Print. 281.

Chapter 5. The Canvas Cathedral

1. Billy Graham, "The Modesto Manifesto: A Declaration of Biblical Integrity." *Billy Graham Evangelistic Association*. BGEA, 24 Oct. 2016. Web. 14 June 2018.

2. William Martin. *A Prophet with Honor: The Billy Graham Story*. Updated ed. Grand Rapids, MI: Zondervan, 2018. Print. 116.

3. David Aikman. *Billy Graham: His Life and Influence*. Nashville: Thomas Nelson, 2007. Print. 69.

4. Aikman, *Billy Graham*, 68.

5. Martin, *A Prophet with Honor*, 119.

6. Martin, *A Prophet with Honor*, 118–119.

7. Martin, *A Prophet with Honor*, 30.

8. Martin, *A Prophet with Honor*, 121, 123.

9. Billy Graham. *Just as I Am: The Autobiography of Billy Graham*. Large print ed. San Francisco: HarperSanFrancisco, 1997. Print. 120.

Chapter 6. *Hour of Decision*

1. William Martin. *A Prophet with Honor: The Billy Graham Story*. Updated ed. Grand Rapids, MI: Zondervan, 2018. Print. 127–128.

2. Billy Graham. *Just as I Am: The Autobiography of Billy Graham*. Large print ed. San Francisco: HarperSanFrancisco, 1997. Print. 235.

3. Brad Tuttle, "Billy Graham Was One of America's Richest Pastors. Here's What We Know about His Money." *Time*. Time, 21 Feb. 2018. Web. 14 June 2018.

4. "Records of the BGEA: World Wide Pictures, Inc.—Collection 214." *Billy Graham Center Archives*. Wheaton College, 2018. Web. 14 June 2018.

5. Martin, *A Prophet with Honor*, 140.

6. Edward B. Fiske, "The Closest Thing to a White House Chaplain." *New York Times*. New York Times, 8 June 1969. Web. 14 June 2018.

7. Martin, *A Prophet with Honor*, 138, 141–142.

8. "The Archives Bulletin Board." *Billy Graham Center Archives*. Wheaton College, 2018. Web. 14 June 2018.

9. Martin, *A Prophet with Honor*, 157–158.

SOURCE NOTES CONTINUED

Chapter 7. Graham and Civil Rights

1. Marshall Frady. *Billy Graham: A Parable of American Righteousness.* Boston: Little, Brown, 1979. Print. 406.

2. David Aikman. *Billy Graham: His Life and Influence.* Nashville: Thomas Nelson, 2007. Print. 138.

3. Billy Graham, "In His Own Words—Billy Graham on Martin Luther King, Jr." *Billy Graham Library.* Billy Graham Evangelistic Association, 18 Jan. 2015. Web. 14 June 2018.

4. William Martin. *A Prophet with Honor: The Billy Graham Story.* Updated ed. Grand Rapids, MI: Zondervan, 2018. Print. 174.

5. *Time Billy Graham: America's Preacher.* Time commemorative ed. New York: Time Books, 2018. Print. 62.

6. John Blake, "Where Billy Graham 'Missed the Mark.'" *CNN.* CNN, 22 Feb. 2018. Web. 14 June 2018.

7. "Birmingham Church Bombing." *History.* A&E Television Networks, 2018. Web. 14 June 2018.

8. Brigit Katz, "Billy Graham, the Evangelical Pastor Who Preached to Millions, Has Died at 99." *Smithsonian.com.* Smithsonian.com, 21 Feb. 2018. Web. 14 June 2018.

Chapter 8. International Ministries

1. John Pollock. *Billy Graham: The Authorized Biography.* New York: McGraw-Hill, 1966. Print. 118.

2. William Martin. *A Prophet with Honor: The Billy Graham Story.* Updated ed. Grand Rapids, MI: Zondervan, 2018. Print. 182.

3. Joanna S. Wong. "Celebrate 50th Anniversary of 'Billy Graham Crusade' in London." *Christianity Today.* Christianity Today, 26 May 2004. Web. 14 June 2018.

4. Martin, *A Prophet with Honor*, 185.

5. Wong, "Celebrate 50th Anniversary."

6. Martin, *A Prophet with Honor*, 204.

7. Patricia Cornwell. *Ruth, a Portrait: The Story of Ruth Bell Graham.* New York: Doubleday, 1997. Print. 164.

8. David Aikman. *Billy Graham: His Life and Influence.* Nashville: Thomas Nelson, 2007. Print. 103.

9. Richard Greene. "Still Looking Up." *Billy Graham Evangelistic Association.* BGEA, 10 Feb. 2011. Web. 14 June 2018.

10. Martin, *A Prophet with Honor*, 422–426.

11. Aikman, *Billy Graham*, 106.

12. "From the Bookshelf of Billy Graham." *Billy Graham Library.* Billy Graham Evangelistic Association, 24 Apr. 2014. Web. 14 June 2018.

13. Marshall Shelley. "Evangelist Billy Graham Has Died." *Christianity Today.* Christianity Today, 2018. Web. 14 June 2018.

14. Martin, *A Prophet with Honor*, 535.

Chapter 9. Advising Presidents

1. "Vietnam War." *History.* A&E Television Networks, 2018. Web. 14 June 2018.

2. William Martin. *A Prophet with Honor: The Billy Graham Story.* Updated ed. Grand Rapids, MI: Zondervan, 2018. Print. 361.

3. Marshall Frady. *Billy Graham: A Parable of American Righteousness.* Boston: Little, Brown, 1979. Print. 438.

4. Dennis Roddy. "The Two Faces of Billy Graham." *Post-Gazette.* Post-Gazette, 9 Mar. 2002. Web. 14 June 2018.

5. Frady, *Billy Graham,* 476–477.

6. Frady, *Billy Graham,* 481.

7. David Aikman. *Billy Graham: His Life and Influence.* Nashville: Thomas Nelson, 2007. Print. 233–234.

8. Martin, *A Prophet with Honor,* 443.

Chapter 10. Finishing the Course

1. Dan Rather. "76: Dan Rather." *Chicken Soup for the Soul.* Chicken Soup for the Soul, 2013. Web. 14 June 2018.

2. Rather, "76: Dan Rather."

3. "Graham's Beliefs: Still Intact." *Christianity Today.* Christianity Today, 13 Jan. 1978. Web. 14 June 2018.

4. Tim Funk and Maria David. "Quotes from Evangelist Billy Graham on Life, Faith, Sin—and His One Regret." *Charlotte Observer.* Charlotte Observer, 21 Feb. 2018. Web. 14 June 2018.

5. David Aikman. *Billy Graham: His Life and Influence.* Nashville: Thomas Nelson, 2007. Print. 258.

6. Aikman, *Billy Graham,* 262.

7. Billy Graham. *Just as I Am: The Autobiography of Billy Graham.* Large print ed. San Francisco: HarperSanFrancisco, 1997. Print. 734.

8. Aikman, *Billy Graham,* 267.

9. "Franklin Graham: Profile: The Prodigal Son Comes Home." *CNN.* CNN, 2001. Web. 14 June 2018.

10. William Martin. *A Prophet with Honor: The Billy Graham Story.* Updated ed. Grand Rapids, MI: Zondervan, 2018. Print. 662–667.

11. "About Anne Graham Lotz." *Anne Graham Lotz AnGeL Ministries.* Anne Graham Lotz/AnGeL Ministries, 2018. Web. 14 June 2018.

12. Aikman, *Billy Graham,* 11.

13. LifeWay Research. "Study Shows Far-Reaching Impact of Billy Graham." *Baptist Press.* Baptist Press, 21 Feb. 2018. Web. 13 Mar. 2018.

14. David Van Biema. "Billy Graham, the Father of Modern Christian Evangelism, Dies at 99." *Time.* Yahoo, 21 Feb. 2018. Web. 14 June 2018.

15. Jon Meacham. "Pilgrim's Progress." *Newsweek.* Newsweek, 13 Aug. 2006. Web. 14 June 2018.

16. Marshall Frady. *Billy Graham: A Parable of American Righteousness.* Boston: Little, Brown, 1979. Print. 316–317.

17. Andy Newman. "Graham Ends Crusade in City Urging Repentance and Hope." *New York Times.* New York Times, 27 June 2005. Web. 14 June 2018.

18. "Billy Graham's Final Crusade." *Billy Graham Library.* Billy Graham Evangelistic Association, 2 Mar. 2018. Web. 14 June 2018.

19. Caleb Lindgren. "Someday You Will Read or Hear That Billy Graham Didn't Really Say That." *Christianity Today.* Christianity Today, 21 Feb. 2108. Web. 14 June 2018.

INDEX

ABOUT THE AUTHOR

Michael Capek is a former English and journalism teacher and the author of numerous books for teens and young adults. When he was growing up, his parents enjoyed listening to Billy Graham's *Hour of Decision* radio programs and rarely missed one of his televised crusade broadcasts.